IN RECITAL®
with Christmas Favorites

ABOUT THE SERIES • A NOTE TO THE TEACHER

In Recital® with Christmas Favorites is devoted to wonderful Christmas repertoire. The fine composers and arrangers of this series have created engaging arrangements of timeless treasures, which have been carefully leveled to ensure success with this repertoire. We know that to motivate, the teacher must challenge the student with attainable goals. This series makes that possible while also providing a perfect holiday treat for your students. You will find favorites that are easy to sing along with, as well as recital-style arrangements of Christmas classics. You will also find some new Christmas gems. This series complements other FJH publications, and will help you plan student recital repertoire for holiday season recitals. The books include CDs with complete performances as well as "play along" tracks designed to assist with recital preparation. Throughout this series you will find a charming history of each Christmas carol researched by Miriam Littell.

 Use the enclosed CD as a teaching and motivational tool. For a guide to using the CD, turn to page 52.

The editor wishes to thank the following people: Miriam Littell, for her superb research on the history of these Christmas carols; Kevin Olson and Robert Schultz; recording producer, Brian Balmages; production coordinators, Philip Groeber and Isabel Otero Bowen; and the publisher, Frank J. Hackinson, whose expertise and commitment to excellence makes books such as these possible.

Production: Frank J. Hackinson
Production Coordinators: Philip Groeber and Isabel Otero Bowen
Art Direction: Terpstra Design, San Francisco – in collaboration with Helen Marlais
Cover and Inside Illustrations: Kevin Hawkes
Engraving: Tempo Music Press, Inc.
Printer: Tempo Music Press, Inc.

ISBN-13: 978-1-56939-536-3

ORGANIZATION OF THE SERIES
IN RECITAL® WITH CHRISTMAS FAVORITES

The series is carefully leveled into the following six categories: Early Elementary, Elementary, Late Elementary, Early Intermediate, Intermediate, and Late Intermediate. Each of the works has been selected for its artistic as well as pedagogical merit.

Book Six — Late Intermediate, reinforces the following concepts:

- Rhythmic patterns of dotted eighth notes, triplets, and sixteenth notes.

- Pieces in simple, compound, and mixed meters.

- More challenging passage work, one octave and two-octave scales, octaves, rolled chords, and hand-over-hand configurations.

- An introduction to the rhythms and style of Spanish music.

- Pieces with changes of key, time signatures, tempo, character, and articulations.

- Students play pieces in which the melody and the accompaniment are found within the same hand.

- A variety of arpeggiated and broken-chord patterns.

- Simple ornamentation is used such as grace notes and trills.

- Pieces reinforce the following musical terms: *espressivo, più mosso, meno mosso, poco a poco dim., rallentando,* along with basic musical terminology found in books 1-5.

- A mixture of major and minor keys strengthen a student's command of the piano.

Dance of the Sugar Plum Fairy, and the medley entitled, *Tres Villancicos (Three Christmas Carols)* were arranged as equal-part duets.

TABLE OF CONTENTS

ABOUT THE CAROLS

Christmas carols were introduced into church services by St. Francis of Assisi 900 years ago in Italy!

Assisi, Italy

What Child Is This

This carol uses the tune from the well-known English folk song titled *Greensleeves*. This folk song, composed 500 years ago, was an English air that was so popular that William Shakespeare mentioned it in *The Merry Wives of Windsor*. The lyrics for *What Child Is This* were written by the Englishman William Chatterton Dix around 1865. It is not known when exactly the lyrics and the music were paired, but they are now an important part of the Christmas holiday season.

Deck the Halls

The Christmas season is one of joyous anticipation of the coming birth of the Christ child. This energetic song about caroling and merrymaking celebrates the happiness and cheerfulness of the season. This is an old Welsh air of folk origins, which may have been created 500 years ago. 300 years ago, the great master Wolfgang Amadeus Mozart (1756-1791) used it in a duet for piano and violin. The first known printing of the lyrics was in New York in 1881.

ABOUT THE CAROLS

O Come, Little Children

This nineteenth century German song, "Ihr Kinderlein, kommet" is a beloved part of the German Christmas season. The words were created by Christoph von Schmid, a German, Roman Catholic priest and schoolmaster who wrote children's literature, and published Bible stories. This song was written around 1850, toward the end of his life. Sometime between 1787 and 1795, his verses were set to a melody by Johann Abraham Peter Schulz, a composer who probably wrote the tune during an appointment to the court of the King of Denmark.

We Three Kings of Orient Are

This Christmas carol, probably the best known song about the three Wise Men, tells the biblical story (Matthew 2:1-11) of the three Wise Men who brought precious and rare gifts of gold, frankincense, and myrrh to the Christ child. John Henry Hopkins created the words and music in 1857, probably in New York City. The song was a big success with the composer's entire family. Its popularity spread, and it was soon published.

Joy to the World

The lyrics to this magnificent hymn celebrating the birth of Christ were composed in England by Isaac Watts (1674-1748), and published in 1719. Watts was a pastor, preacher, poet, and prolific hymn writer. He and Charles Wesley are revered authors of Christian hymns. The American music educator Lowell Mason (1792-1872) wrote the music for *Joy to the World* in the style of George Frideric Handel. It was published in 1839, and is often attributed to Handel.

The Twelve Days of Christmas

This song uses the centuries-old tradition of counting in nursery rhymes. It features animals, which children always enjoy! The twelve days of Christmas are the period between Christmas Eve and Epiphany, when the Wise Men visited Christ in the manger. This song is of English folk origin—probably created around 400 years ago, and published around 1780.

What Child Is This

(Greensleeves)

Words: William Chatterton Dix   Music: English Folk Song
arr. Kevin Costley

With movement and vitality (♩ = ca. 120)

FJH1578

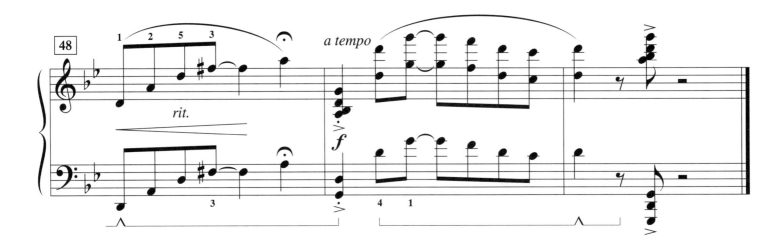

What child is this who, laid to rest, on Mary's lap is sleeping?
Whom angels greet with anthems sweet, while shepherds watch are keeping?
This, this is Christ the King, whom shepherds guard and angels sing:
Haste, haste, to bring Him laud, the Babe, the Son of Mary.

FJH1578

Deck the Halls

16th Century Welsh Carol   arr. Robert Schultz

With spirit (♩ = ca. 92)

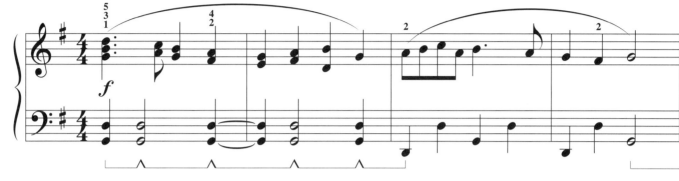

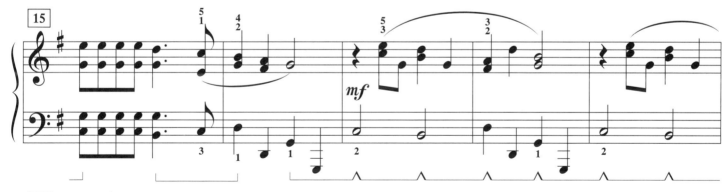

O Come, Little Children

J.A.P. Schulz   arr. Melody Bober

Flowing (♩ = ca. 100)

This arrangement © 2005 The FJH Music Company Inc. (ASCAP).

FJH1578

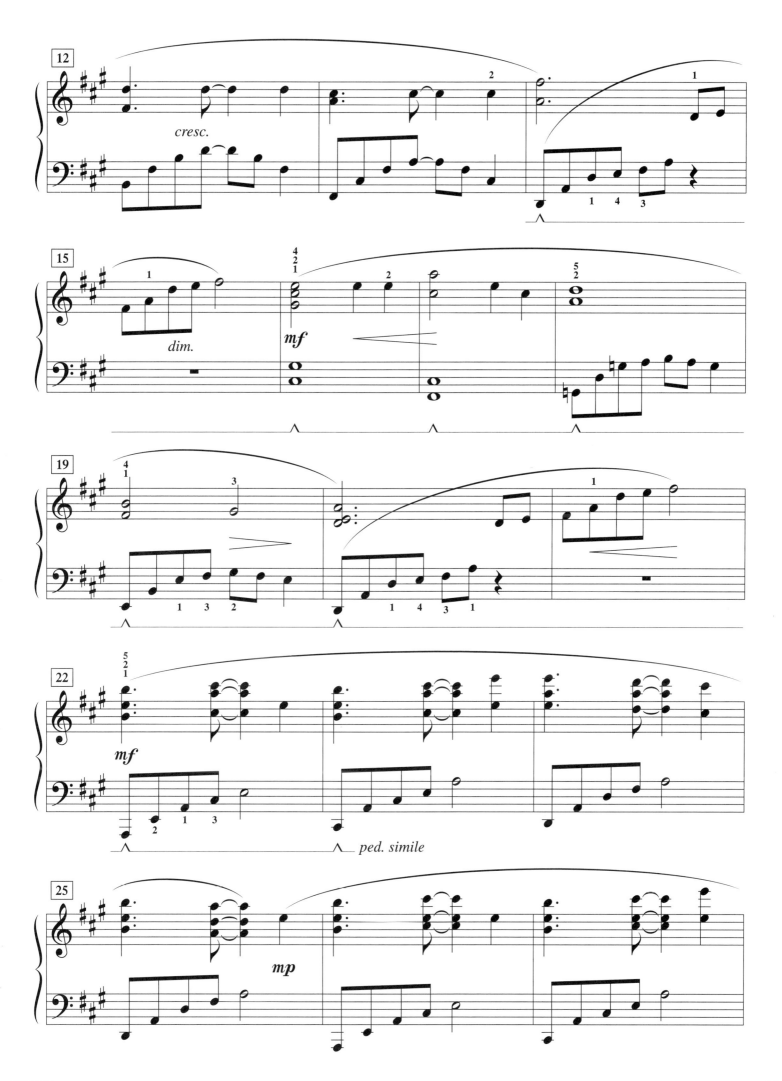

We Three Kings of Orient Are

John H. Hopkins, Jr.   arr. Kevin Costley

Joy to the World

Lowell Mason   arr. Edwin McLean

Joyful and spirited (♩ = ca. 100)

FJH1578

A Christmas Fantasy

based on *The Twelve Days of Christmas*

Old English Carol   arr. Timothy Brown

FJH1578

Away in a Manger

Words: Traditional   Music: Jonathan E. Spilman   arr. Robert Schultz

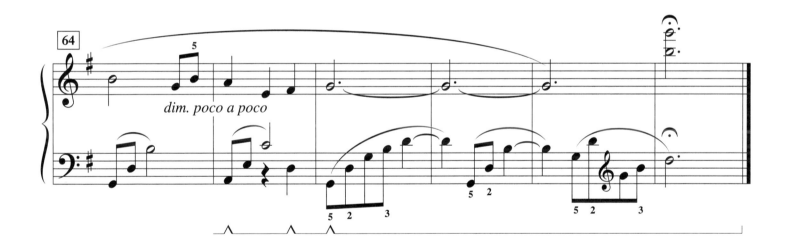

Away in a manger no crib for a bed,
The little Lord Jesus laid down His sweet head.
The stars in the sky looked down where He lay,
The little Lord Jesus asleep on the hay.

Dance of the Sugar Plum Fairy

from *The Nutcracker Suite*

Secondo

Pyotr (Peter) Ilyich Tchaikovsky　　arr. Timothy Brown

FJH1578

Dance of the Sugar Plum Fairy

from *The Nutcracker Suite*

Primo

Pyotr (Peter) Ilyich Tchaikovsky   arr. Timothy Brown

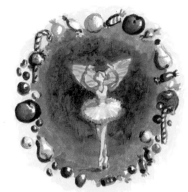

Secondo

Primo

Silent Night
(Stille Nacht)

Words: Joseph Mohr, English Translation by John F. Young
Music: Franz Gruber   arr. Melody Bober

FJH1578

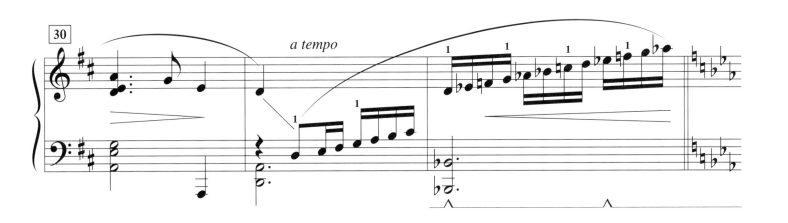

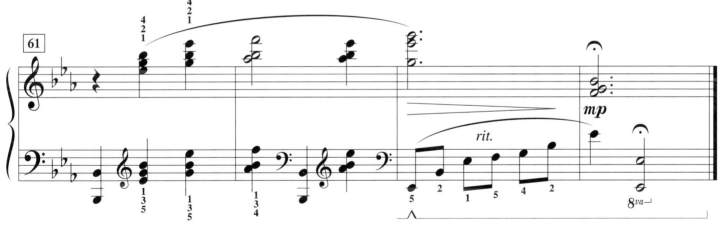

Silent night, holy night, all is calm, all is bright,
'Round yon Virgin Mother and child.
Holy infant so tender and mild.
Sleep in heavenly peace. Sleep in heavenly peace!

Tres Villancicos
(Three Christmas Carols)
Secondo

Los peces en el río: Traditional Spanish Carol
A la nanita nana: Traditional Spanish Carol
Campana sobre campana: Traditional Andalucian Carol   arr. Kevin Olson

Los peces en el río

With energy and passion (♩ = 108-112)

FJH1578

Tres Villancicos
(*Three Christmas Carols*)
Primo

Los peces en el río: Traditional Spanish Carol
A la nanita nana: Traditional Spanish Carol
Campana sobre campana: Traditional Andalucian Carol   arr. Kevin Olson

Los peces en el río

With energy and passion (♩ = 108-112)

Secondo

FJH1578

Primo

A la nanita nana

Smoothly ($\quarternote = 120$)

Secondo

Primo

Secondo

Primo

Auld Lang Syne

Words: Robert Burns   Music: Traditional Scottish Melody   arr. Melody Bober

Reflective, freely (♩ = 76-80)

FJH1578

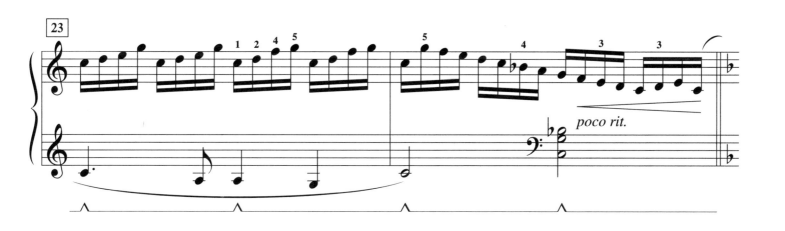

Broader (♩ = 72-84)

FJH1578

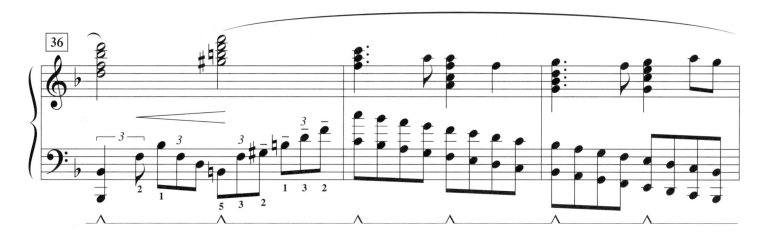

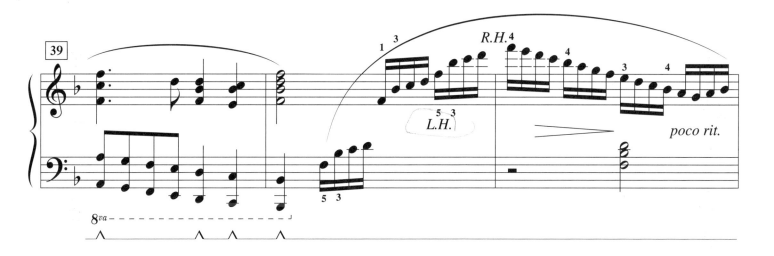

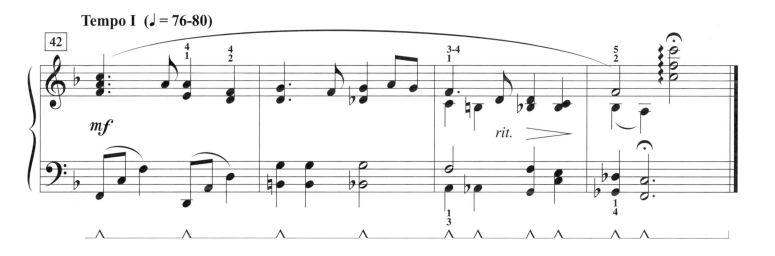

Should auld acquaintance be forgot, And never brought to mind?
Should auld acquaintance be forgot, And days of auld lang syne!
For auld lang syne, my dear, For auld lang syne.
We'll take a cup o' kindness yet, For days of auld lang syne.

ABOUT THE CAROLS

Away in a Manger

For many years, the important historical religious figure Martin Luther was incorrectly considered the author of the words to this song. The lyrics were first published in 1885, and are now thought to have come from the German Lutheran community of Pennsylvania. Jonathan E. Spilman (1812-1896) composed the melody, and it was originally written for the Scottish song, *Flow Gently, Sweet Afton*.

Dance of the Sugar Plum Fairy

This piece comes from the ballet called *The Nutcracker*, written by Pyotr Ilyich Tchaikovsky in 1892. The story is about a little girl who receives a nutcracker doll as a gift. When she dreams in the night that her nutcracker has turned into a handsome prince, they escape an army of mice through the magical lands of the Snow Queen and the Sugar Plum Fairy. In this dance, Tchaikovsky introduced the "celesta," an instrument he had just discovered in Paris, which he described to his publisher as "something between a piano and a glockenspiel, with a divinely beautiful tone."

Silent Night *(Stille Nacht)*

This most beloved of all German carols was first performed in a little church in the beautiful Tyrol region of lakes and mountains on the border of Austria and Bavaria in 1818. On Christmas Eve, church organist Franz Gruber found his organ out of order. He and the assistant priest, Joseph Mohr, quickly composed lyrics and an original melody for two voices and a choir with guitar accompaniment for the service. The song was first published in 1838, and by 1955 it was the most recorded song of all time.

FJH1578

ABOUT THE CAROLS

Tres Villancicos *(Three Christmas Carols)*

Los peces en el río

This is one of the most popular Spanish Christmas carols, although it is not well known outside the Spanish-speaking world. This charming song, of anonymous origins, tells of the fish in the river delighting over the birth of the Savior, while Mary tends to her baby and her daily chores.

A la nanita nana

The lyrics and music to this Spanish carol are of folk origin, and were created sometime between the sixteenth and eighteenth centuries. This carol combines a tender lullaby with a melody and rhythms of popular Latin authenticity. The melody is hauntingly beautiful, with a change from a minor to a major key.

Campana sobre campana *(Bells Over Bethlehem)*

This traditional Spanish carol comes from the region of Andalusia, on the Atlantic Ocean and the Mediterranean Sea in southern Spain. The music and lyrics are of folk origin, created between the seventeenth and nineteenth centuries. The song is known in English as *Bells Over Bethlehem*, and was translated by George K. Evans.

Auld Lang Syne

It has become a New Year's Eve tradition to ring out the old year and bring in the new with this old Scotch folk song. These lyrics were composed by Robert Burns in 1788, although additional verses, anonymously written, have been found. The music is traditional Scottish folk music, dating between 500 and 700 years ago. The tune and the verses first appeared together in 1799. *Auld Lang Syne*, translated from the Scottish, means "old long since," so the song is a chance to look affectionately on times past and be sure they are not forgotten.

ABOUT THE ARRANGERS

Melody Bober

Piano instructor, music teacher, composer, clinician—Melody Bober has been active in music education for over 25 years. As a composer, her goal is to create exciting and challenging pieces that are strong teaching tools to promote a lifelong love, understanding, and appreciation for music. Pedagogy, ear training, and musical expression are fundamentals of Melody's teaching, as well as fostering composition skills in her students.

Melody graduated with highest honors from the University of Illinois with a degree in music education, and later received a master's degree in piano performance. She maintains a large private studio, performs in numerous regional events, and conducts workshops across the country. She and her husband Jeff reside in Minnesota.

Timothy Brown

Timothy Brown holds a master's degree in piano performance from the University of North Texas, where he studied piano with Adam Wodnicki and music composition with Newel Kay Brown. He was later a recipient of a research fellowship from the Royal Holloway, University of London, where he performed postgraduate studies in music composition and orchestration, studying with English composer Brian Lock.

His numerous credits as a composer include first prize at the Aliénor International Harpsichord Competition for his harpsichord solo *Suite Española* (Centaur Records). Mr. Brown leads a very active career as an exclusive composer and clinician for The FJH Music Company Inc.

Mr. Brown's works have been performed by concert artist Elaine Funaro on NPR, and most recently at the Spoleto Music Festival and the Library of Congress Concert Series in Washington, D.C. His numerous commissions include a commission by *Clavier* Magazine for his piano solo *Once Upon a Time*, edited by Denes Agay. Mr. Brown is currently a fine arts specialist for the Dallas Public Schools and serves on the advisory board of the Booker T. Washington High School for the Performing and Visual Arts in Dallas, Texas.

Kevin Costley

Kevin Costley holds several graduate degrees in the areas of elementary education and piano pedagogy, and literature, including a doctorate from Kansas State University. For nearly two decades, he was owner and director of The Keyboard Academy, specializing in innovative small group instruction. Kevin served for several years as head of the music department and on the keyboard faculty of Messenger College in Joplin, Missouri.

Kevin is a standing faculty member of Inspiration Point Fine Arts Colony piano and string camp, where he performs and teaches private piano, ensemble classes, and composition. He conducts child development seminars, writes for national publications, serves as a clinician for piano workshops, and adjudicates numerous piano festivals and competitions. Presently, Dr. Costley is an associate professor of early childhood education at Arkansas Tech University in Russellville, Arkansas.

Edwin McLean

Edwin McLean is a composer living in Chapel Hill, North Carolina. He is a graduate of the Yale School of Music, where he studied with Krzysztof Penderecki and Jacob Druckman. He also holds a master's degree in music theory and a bachelor's degree in piano performance from the University of Colorado.

Mr. McLean has been the recipient of several grants and awards: The MacDowell Colony, the John Work Award, the Woods Chandler Prize (Yale), Meet the Composer, Florida Arts Council, and many others. He has also won the Aliénor Composition Competition for his work *Sonata for Harpsichord*, published by The FJH Music Company Inc. and recorded by Elaine Funaro (*Into the Millennium*, Gasparo GSCD-331). His complete works for harpsichord are available on the Miami Bach Society recording, *Edwin McLean: Sonatas for 1, 2, and 3 Harpsichords*.

Since 1979, Edwin McLean has arranged the music of some of today's best-known recording artists. Currently, he is senior editor for The FJH Music Company Inc.

Kevin Olson

Kevin Olson is an active pianist, composer, and member of the piano faculty at Utah State University, where he teaches piano literature, pedagogy, and accompanying courses. In addition to his collegiate teaching responsibilities, Kevin directs the Utah State Youth Conservatory, which provides weekly group and private piano instruction to more than 200 pre-college, community students. The National Association of Schools of Music has recently recognized the Utah State Youth Conservatory as a model for pre-college piano instruction programs. Before teaching at Utah State, he was on the faculty at Elmhurst College near Chicago and Humboldt State University in northern California.

A native of Utah, Kevin began composing at age five. When he was twelve, his composition, An American Trainride, received the Overall First Prize at the 1983 National PTA Convention at Albuquerque, New Mexico. Since then he has been a Composer in Residence at the National Conference on Piano Pedagogy, and has written music commissioned and performed by groups such as the American Piano Quartet, Chicago a cappella, the Rich Matteson Jazz Festival, and several piano teacher associations around the country. He holds a Doctor of Education degree from National-Louis University, and a bachelor's and a master's degree in music composition from Brigham Young University. Kevin maintains a large piano studio, teaching students of a variety of ages and abilities. Many of the needs of his own piano students have inspired more than 100 books and solos published by The FJH Music Company, which he joined as a writer in 1994.

Robert Schultz

Robert Schultz, composer, arranger, and editor, has achieved international fame during his career in the music publishing industry. The Schultz Piano Library, established in 1980, has included more than 500 publications of classical works, popular arrangements, and Schultz's original compositions in editions for pianists of every level from the beginner through the concert artist. In addition to his extensive library of published piano works, Schultz's output includes original orchestral works, chamber music, works for solo instruments, and vocal music.

Schultz has presented his published editions at workshops, clinics, and convention showcases throughout the United States and Canada. He is a long-standing member of ASCAP and has served as president of the Miami Music Teachers Association. Mr. Schultz's original piano compositions and transcriptions are featured on the compact disc recordings *Visions of Dunbar* and *Tina Faigen Plays Piano Transcriptions*, released on the ACA Digital label and available worldwide. His published original works for concert artists are noted in Maurice Hinson's *Guide to the Pianist's Repertoire, Third Edition*. He currently devotes his full time to composing and arranging, writing from his studio in Miami, Florida.

USING THE CD

A great way to prepare for your Christmas recitals is to use the CD in the following ways:

1) The first 11 tracks are the solo piano performances of each Christmas carol. Enjoy listening to these pieces anywhere anytime! Listen to them casually (as background music) and attentively. Follow along with your score as you listen and after you have finished listening, you might discuss interpretation with your teacher.

2) The rest of the tracks are to help you prepare for your Christmas recitals. The CD can be used as a practice partner, because you can play along with the tracks! This is how it works: Each carol has two accompaniment tracks. The first accompaniment track is for practice. It is at a slower tempo so that you can learn to play with the accompaniment. You will hear your part along with the accompaniment. You can play hands separately or hands together. The second version of the accompaniment is the "performance-ready" track. It is *a tempo* and does not include your part. All it needs to make it complete is your piano playing!

In both versions, before the accompaniment begins, you will hear a steady beat for two measures so that you know the tempo.

All of the CD orchestrations were created by Dr. Kevin Olson on a Roland KR-7 piano.

FJH1578